THE CALL
OF THE WILD

The Call of the Wild

JACK LONDON

Adapted by
Ardis E. Burton

Edited by
William Kottmeyer
St. Louis Public Schools

Illustrated by
Bill Macnamee

Phoenix Learning Resources
New York

The Phoenix Everyreaders

The EVERYREADERS were selected from the great literature of the world and adapted to the needs of today's children. This series retains the flavor of the originals, providing mature content and dramatic plot structure, along with eye appeal designed to motivate reading.

This approach was first developed in the renowned St. Louis Reading Clinic by Dr. Kottmeyer and is the direct outgrowth of wide and successful teaching of remedial reading.

A high interest level plus the carefully controlled vocabulary and sentence structure enable pupils to read the stories easily, confidently, and with enjoyment.

ISBN 0–7915–1363–7

3 4 5 6 7 8 9 0 99 98 97 96 95 94

Contents

CHAPTER 1

Trouble Comes for Buck

Trouble was coming for Buck, Judge Miller's big dog. He was in great danger, but he did not know it.

The year was 1897. Gold had been found in Alaska, and the gold rush was on. Along the Yukon, a river in Alaska, thousands of men were digging for gold. Thousands more were rushing to the Yukon to make money. These men needed big, strong dogs with thick coats. In Alaska strong dogs did the heavy work. Teams of dogs pulled sleds over the snow.

All over the West, dogs were being stolen, sold, and sent to Alaska. Buck and every other big dog in the West was in danger.

Buck's father was a big St. Bernard. His mother was a shepherd. Buck was four years

1

old and weighed one hundred and forty pounds.

Buck lived in California on the Miller ranch, where he had been born. He was a big outdoor dog with a strong body and long, thick fur. He hunted with Judge Miller's sons and ran freely over the ranch. Everyone loved him. Everyone, that is, but one of Judge Miller's workers.

This man, named Manuel, worked in the garden. He had lost much money gambling, and he needed cash. He knew he could get a good price for Buck, and he planned to steal the big dog.

One dark night Manuel called, "Come, Buck, come with me."

Buck had been sleeping on the porch. He got up, ready to go for a walk.

They went down the path and out the gate. No one saw them leave. Buck followed Manuel across the field.

They walked for two or three miles. At last they came to a corner where a stranger was waiting for them. The two men talked and the stranger gave Manuel some money.

"Why didn't you put a rope around his neck?" asked the strange man. "He looks as if he will be hard to hold."

"I have some rope," said Manuel. "Here it is."

He took some strong rope from under his coat. He tied it around Buck's neck.

"Just twist the rope if you have to," said Manuel. "If you choke him, he'll behave!"

Buck had never had a rope around his neck before. He had learned to trust the men he knew, and he trusted Manuel. No one had ever treated him badly. He did not know what was in store for him.

When Buck saw Manuel hand the rope to the stranger, he knew something was wrong. He growled a warning. The stranger twisted the rope until it was tight around Buck's neck. He couldn't breathe. Buck sprang for the man's neck. The man threw out his arm and struck Buck down. Then he tightened the rope.

Buck fought wildly. He panted and gasped for air. The big dog was being choked to death, and his strength was soon gone. His eyes became glassy, and he sank to the ground. Before long a train stopped near the corner. The men lifted Buck and threw the half-dead dog into the baggage car.

When Buck came to, the train was rolling over the tracks. For a moment, he wondered where he was. Then he heard the train whistle. He knew then that he was in a baggage car, as he often had been with Judge Miller.

Buck's mouth and neck hurt. He felt sore. When he opened his eyes and saw the stranger, he roared and jumped for him. The stranger tried to hold him, but Buck was too quick. Catching the man's hand in his mouth, he tore it with his sharp teeth. But the stranger pulled on the rope and choked Buck until he again passed out.

The baggage man heard the noise and ran into the car. "What's the matter with your dog?" he asked.

"He has fits," the man said. "I'm taking him to a vet in San Francisco."

The stranger wrapped his bleeding hand in his handkerchief. He held the rope tight around Buck's throat. At last the train stopped near the waterfront in San Francisco. Buck spent the night in a shed near the tracks.

In the morning, Buck's head and body were sore. He could not understand what was happening. Never before had anyone hurt him.

"How much did you get for stealing him?" a man asked the stranger.

"I got only fifty dollars," the stranger said. "And I wouldn't do it again for a thousand!"

He held out his hand, which was tied up in bloody rags.

"How much did Manuel get?" the man asked.

"He got a hundred dollars."

"One hundred and fifty dollars for a dog!" cried the man. "But from the looks of this one, he was well worth it. He seems to be a fine dog."

"Fine dog!" said the man. "He's a wild beast!"

The other man laughed. Then he said, "If you want, I'll help you load him."

Buck faced the men. He fought to free himself. But over and over again they threw him down and choked him. Then they pushed him into a big wooden box. They took the rope off his neck.

Buck lay there the rest of the night. He was angry and he hurt.

What did these men want with him? Why wouldn't they let him go? Where were Judge Miller and the boys?

Buck knew that something was wrong. He sensed that worse things were ahead. He growled angrily.

CHAPTER 2

The Dog-Breaker

In the morning, four dirty, ragged men came into the shed. Buck growled when they came toward the box.

The four men laughed and poked him with sticks. They teased him and made him rage and throw himself against the wooden bars.

Then they lifted the box into a wagon, and Buck began another long trip. He was moved from one place to another, and many different men took care of him.

He rode trains, wagons, trucks, and boats. He rode on the last train for two days and nights without anything to eat.

The men who worked on the trains all teased him. They laughed at him when he tried to get out of the cage.

Buck was very hungry and thirsty. The long days and nights made him grow more and more wild.

At last the train got to Seattle, Washington. Four men pulled his box off the train. They were glad to be rid of him, for he was no longer a gentle dog. He had become a wild animal.

The men set Buck's box down in a yard. Around the yard was a wall too high for him to jump. A big man with a red sweater came over to the cage. Buck knew this man was his next enemy. Throwing himself against the bars, Buck barked and growled.

"This is a good time to take him out," the man in the red sweater said.

Holding a hatchet and a club, he walked toward Buck's box. He drove the hatchet into the wood and pulled the bars apart.

The other men got on top of the wall. They wanted to watch from a safe place.

Buck rushed at the bars of his cage. He sank his teeth into the wood.

"Come on, you devil!" cried the man, dropping the hatchet and grabbing the club.

Buck's hair stood on end, his mouth foamed, and his eyes were red. He looked like a mad dog. Buck leaped for the man in the red sweater. For two days and nights he had saved up for this. Now he attacked.

Buck was in mid-air. Just when his jaws were about to close, the man hit him with the club. He fell to the ground. He turned over, jumped to his feet, and leaped again.

The man hit him with the club, and again Buck fell to the ground. He charged time after time. Time after time the man smashed him down. Buck once more got to his feet. He was limp. Blood ran from his nose, his mouth, and his ears and dripped onto his beautiful coat.

The man walked toward him, raised his club, and brought it down hard on Buck's nose. Buck screamed in pain and anger. Again he threw himself at the man in the red sweater. The man clubbed him over and over. Buck crashed to the ground for the last time. He lay senseless.

"That dog's a fighter!" cried one of the men on the wall.

"What chance does he have against a club?" said another.

"That fellow is good at breaking dogs, I say," said another.

"I'd rather break horses, any day," said the fourth man watching.

Buck opened his eyes. He felt weak. He could not move. He lay where he had fallen, but his eyes followed the man in the red sweater.

"They say your name is Buck," the man said. "Well, Buck, my boy, we had to have it out. Now we know who is boss. You keep your place, and I'll keep mine. If you're a good dog, everything will be fine."

He leaned over the dog and patted him. Buck hated the feel of his hand. But he could do nothing.

The man got him a pan of water, and Buck drank. Later he ate a big meal of raw meat from the man's hand.

Buck knew that he was beaten. He knew that he had no chance against a man with a club. This was a lesson he would never forget. He knew that his life had changed, but he was not afraid. He was smart enough to learn quickly. These bad men were teaching him many things.

As the days went by, more and more dogs were put into the pen with Buck. Some came without a fight. Some came roaring and raging, as Buck had come. Buck watched them all. He watched the man with the club.

The man knew the dogs had been stolen, but he sold the dogs. Strangers came, bought dogs, and took them away. Buck wondered where they went. He was glad each time that he was not taken.

But Buck's turn came, too. A thin little man came to the pen. His eyes lit up when he saw Buck.

"That big dog looks like a good one for me," he said. "How much do you want for him?"

"Three hundred dollars," said the man in the red sweater. "He's worth every cent of it."

The price of dogs was very high. Big, strong dogs were hard to get. The men had to have them and had to pay.

"You're with the Canadian government, aren't you?" asked the dog-breaker.

"That's right," said the little man. "Three hundred dollars is too much for any dog. But the government needs good dogs. They won't lose on Buck."

Buck saw the little man pay the man in the red sweater. The little man also paid for Curly, a gentle Newfoundland. Curly and Buck were led away. That was the last Buck ever saw of the man in the red sweater.

It was also the last he ever saw of the United States. Soon he and Curly were on the deck of a ship headed for Alaska.

Day and night the ship sailed north. One day was just like another. Buck, Curly, and two other dogs ate and slept below deck. Sometimes they fought over their food, but the man would stop the fight with his whip. Buck did not try to steal food. He wanted only to be left alone.

Each day the wind grew colder.

At last, one morning, the ship came to Alaska. The people on the boat got ready to land.

A man came down below deck, put straps on the big dogs, and took them off the ship.

Buck was glad to be on land again. His feet sank into deep snow. He had never seen snow before and did not know what it was. He jumped back.

More snow was falling. It fell on Buck's thick, long fur. He shook himself. He sniffed it. It had no smell. Then he tasted it. He licked it again and again. Then men who were standing around watching him laughed. Buck did not like to be laughed at. He hated the men for laughing at him.

CHAPTER 3

The Law of
Club and Fang

The day the ship landed in Alaska was a bad one for Buck. Only a short time before, he had been living on a California ranch. The long, lazy days had been happy ones.

Now he was living in a wild, faraway place. There was no peace. There was no safety. There was no law but the law of club and fang. Only the strongest could live.

Buck had never seen such wolf-like dogs or such bloody fights. He soon learned another lesson he would never forget. Curly, who came with him on the ship, had to lose her life.

Curly, in her friendly way, tried to make friends with Spitz, a smaller dog. Spitz leaped like a flash. He ripped Curly's face open from her eye to her jaw. Thirty or forty more dogs came running. They sat in a ring

around Curly and Spitz. They watched and waited, licking their lips. Curly rushed her enemy. But Spitz struck again, slashed her, and leaped away. Then he knocked her off her feet. This was what the other dogs were waiting for.

They closed in on poor Curly. Snarling and yelping, they piled on top of her. She was screaming with pain. But they tore her to bits. She was buried under their bodies. They tore at her like starving wolves.

A man jumped into the middle of the snarling, fighting dogs. It took three more men with clubs to get them apart. Curly lay dead. Her body was stamped into the snow. She was torn almost apart. Buck never forgot that fight.

So that was the way of this new land. Once down, that was the end of you. Buck always hated Spitz for what he had done.

A big half-breed named Frank took care of the dogs. One day he took a harness to the pen and put it on Buck.

Buck had seen work horses harnessed at the ranch. Frank harnessed Buck in the same way. He showed Buck and the other dogs how to pull a sled over the snow. With Frank riding the sled, they went to the woods for loads of firewood. Buck did not like this work. But he did his very best.

Frank was strict with the dogs, and Buck soon learned to obey. Dave was the dog who ran behind Buck. If Buck did something wrong, Dave nipped his heels. Spitz, the leader, jerked Buck around to go the right way.

Buck soon learned how to work in the sled team. He learned to stop when Frank yelled "Ho!" He learned to go ahead when he said "Mush!" He learned to swing wide at the turns in the trail. He learned to keep ahead of the sled coming down a hill.

"That Buck, he pulls hard," Frank told another man. "He's a very good dog."

One afternoon two huskies were led in. They were brothers, Billy and Joe. A husky is a strong Eskimo dog that makes a good sled dog.

Billy and Joe were as different as day and night. Billy was happy and would not fight.

Joe was cross and snapped at the other dogs. Buck watched Joe and Billy come into the pen. He made no move.

Dave, the "wheel" dog, did not look at the huskies. But Spitz quickly went after both. Billy ran away, but Joe turned to face the bully. Joe's hair rose. He growled and laid his ears flat back on his head. He showed his teeth. His eyes shone wildly. He looked so terrible that Spitz would not fight.

Soon another dog was put in at the gate. This one was named Sol-leks, which means Angry One. He was somewhat like Dave. He asked for nothing. He gave nothing. He looked for nothing. When Sol-leks marched into the pen, even Spitz let him alone.

Sol-leks was blind in one eye. He did not like anyone to come up on his blind side. Buck didn't know this. But he learned quickly when Sol-leks cut his shoulder to the bone for three inches up and down. After this Buck never forgot to keep away from Sol-leks' blind side.

The two dogs became friends. Buck thought Sol-leks only wanted to be left alone.

Later he learned that Sol-leks had another wish, one Buck also had — to be free.

Buck didn't know where to sleep. He liked to sleep outdoors, but the Alaskan night was bitter cold. He tried to sleep in the tent, but Frank saw him. He threw a pan at Buck. Then Frank took the broom and chased Buck back into the cold.

Buck lay down on the snow and tried to sleep, but the icy wind soon drove him to his feet. He walked about sadly.

He wondered where the other dogs were sleeping and went back to find them. To his surprise, he did not see them. Though he looked all over the great camp for them, Buck could not find one dog. Where could they be?

Suddenly the snow gave way under his feet. He sank into a hole. Something moved under his feet. Buck sprang back, snarling and growling. He was always afraid of what he did not understand. Then he heard a friendly yap.

There, curled up under the snow, was Billy. He was as snug and warm as could be.

Billy wagged his tail to show his good wishes to Buck. He even tried to lick Buck's face.

So that was the way the dogs kept warm at night! It was another lesson for Buck. He looked around and found a place. Then he dug a hole for himself. In a short time the heat from his body filled the small hole, and he slept soundly.

CHAPTER 4

On the Trail

Noises from the camp woke him. At first he couldn't remember where he was. Snow had fallen during the night. Buck was buried deep in the snow. He thought he was trapped, and he bounded into the blinding sunshine. Then he remembered everything that had happened.

"What did I tell you?" shouted Frank. "That Buck learns fast."

"He has already learned to dig a hole in the snow," said the other man.

"He'll be a good one on that sled going to the Klondike," said Frank. "He's smart, he's fast, and he's brave."

After breakfast, the nine-dog team was harnessed. Soon they were trotting along the trail. This was hard work, but Buck liked it.

The team's hard work surprised Buck. All the dogs were ready to go at any time. They seemed happy to work together as a team. They loved to pull the sled.

Buck was surprised at the change in Dave and Sol-leks. They seemed like different dogs.

Dave was the wheeler, or sled-dog, the last one in line. Pulling in front of him was Buck. Then came Sol-leks. The rest of the team was out ahead, in a line. Spitz was in the lead.

Buck had been put between Dave and Sol-leks because they were good teachers. When he did something wrong they nipped him with their sharp teeth. Dave, the sled dog, was fair and wise. Buck found it easier to do the right thing than to be bitten, and he learned fast.

Once, when the sled was ready to start, Buck got tangled in the lines. Dave and Sol-leks jumped on him and whipped him. After that, he was more careful. Before the day was over, he had learned his work. The other dogs no longer had to bite him. That night Frank lifted up Buck's feet and checked them. Buck knew that Frank liked him.

It was a hard day's run up the trail. They went across ice and snowdrifts hundreds of feet deep. They crossed the great mountains which guard the lonely North. Then they passed a chain of rocky hills. After going forty miles, they came to a big camp at Lake Bennett.

Buck dug a hole in the snow. He slept soundly, for he was very tired. It seemed that he had just shut his eyes when morning came.

After the first day, the sled dogs went slower. The men had to break the ice on the trail. Frank guided the sled at the gee-pole. Perrault, the other man, went ahead, breaking the trail for the dog team and packing it with his snowshoes.

Day after day, Buck worked with the other dogs. They broke camp before it was light, and were on their way in the first gray light of dawn. They never made camp until after dark.

Buck was always very hungry. Each day he ate a pound and a half of dried salmon. But it was never enough for him.

In the old days, Buck had taken his time about meals. He had eaten with good manners. Now it was different. He found that the dogs that ate first robbed the others. While Buck was fighting off the first dogs, other dogs would take his food. Soon he ate as fast as any. Sometimes he even took another dog's food. Buck was learning many things.

One day he saw Pike, a new dog, steal a piece of bacon. The next day Buck did the same thing, getting away with a big chunk. A great fight followed. But nobody knew Buck had done it. Dub, another dog, was beaten.

Buck showed that he was going to get along in the far North. He did not like this kind of life. But since he had to live here, he could change his ways. He could learn the law of club and fang.

Buck grew as hard as iron. Now he hardly felt pain. He could eat anything, and it agreed with him. His eyes and nose became very keen.

He learned to bite the ice from between his toes with his teeth. He learned to break the ice to get drinking water. He learned to sniff the wind before he went to sleep. In the morning, he was always in a warm hole. He had almost forgotten the happy days in California.

Buck's wild feelings, long dead, came to life again. Sometimes he acted like the wild dogs, his great-great-grandparents, that ran in packs and hunted their meat in the woods.

Buck learned to fight like a wolf. He learned to cut and slash with his sharp teeth. Sometimes, on a still, cold night, he pointed his nose toward a star and howled. He sometimes looked and sounded just like a wolf.

Sunny California was far away. In this wild land Buck heard the call of the wild for the first time. Something in him wanted to answer it. What would he do?

CHAPTER 5

Trouble Starts

Buck had the blood of wild dogs in his body. The longer he lived on the cold Alaskan trail, the more he began to feel, think, and act as they had. Buck was learning to get along in this new land. He kept to himself and stayed out of fights whenever he could. He hated Spitz, but he stayed away from him.

Spitz knew that sooner or later he and Buck would fight a death battle. Spitz went out of his way to bully the big dog from the south.

One night, caught in a driving snow, Perrault and Frank made camp on the shore of a lake. They had no tent and no wood for a fire. They had to sleep on the ice. Never had they camped in a worse place.

Buck found a warm spot under some rocks. When he had eaten his salmon, he went to this place. But he found Spitz in his soft bed. This was too much for Buck. He roared wildly and sprang at Spitz.

Spitz was surprised, because Buck had always let him alone.

Frank, too, was surprised. He cried, "Give it to him, Buck! Go for him! He's a dirty robber!"

Buck and Spitz went around each other, snarling and looking for a chance to attack. Just at that moment, something happened which put off their fight until another day. This is what it was.

As Buck and Spitz stood ready to fight, the camp was suddenly filled with about a hundred starving, mad dogs. They had smelled Perrault's cooking and had crept into camp before they were seen. The two men grabbed their clubs. One of the strange dogs turned over the food box, and they all fought for the bread and bacon. Frank and Perrault beat them with the heavy clubs, but the starved huskies fought back.

The dogs of the sled team awakened. They had never seen such animals! The huskies looked as if their bones would poke through their ragged fur. Their eyes blazed, and their mouths dripped.

In a moment the wild huskies attacked the sled dogs. Three of them jumped on Buck. They slashed his head and shoulders. The huskies drove the sled dogs against the wall of the cliff.

Billy cried. Dave and Sol-leks fought bravely side by side. Joe snapped the leg of a husky with one bite of his strong teeth. Pike broke the neck of another. Buck grabbed one enemy by the throat and sank his teeth into his neck. The taste of hot blood made him wilder.

Suddenly Buck felt sharp teeth at his own throat. Spitz was attacking him from the other side!

Perrault and Frank rushed to save their dogs. Before them, the huskies fell back. For a moment Buck was able to free himself from Spitz. Then the huskies attacked again. The men ran back to save their food.

Billy, so scared that he acted without thinking, sprang through the ring of starving dogs and ran away over the frozen lake. Pike, Dub, and the others followed at his heels. As Buck started to spring after them, he saw Spitz getting ready to rush him and knock him off his feet. He knew that if he fell there would be no hope for him. Buck saw Spitz just in time to save himself from the attack. Then he went with the others, running over the ice.

Later, the sled dogs met in the woods. Each of them was wounded in many places. Dub's hind leg was badly hurt. Dolly's throat was torn. Joe had lost one eye. Billy, whose ears were chewed to bits, cried with pain all night long.

At dawn the dogs limped back to camp. The starving huskies had gone. Frank and Perrault were angry. The wild pack had eaten more than half of the food. They had chewed through the rawhide straps that held the sled together. They had torn the cover that covered the load. They had even eaten parts of the harness!

"Ah, my friends," Frank said softly to the dog team, "maybe all those cuts will make you mad like those other dogs." He turned to Perrault. "What do you think?"

Perrault shook his head. He did not know. He thought of the four hundred miles they still had to go to Dawson. He did not want to have madness break out among his dogs.

CHAPTER 6

More Trouble

Frank and Perrault worked on the broken harness for two hours. The limping, tired dogs at last got started. They headed for the hardest part of the trail, Thirty-Mile River.

The fast water of Thirty-Mile River was not frozen solid. It took six days of hard work for the team to make those thirty miles!

Perrault himself broke through the ice a dozen times. The only thing that saved him was the long pole that he carried. He held it so that when he broke through the ice the pole would reach across the hole and hold his body up. When he crawled out of the icy water, the two men would build a fire to dry Perrault's clothes.

But nothing scared Perrault. Though he was small, he was very brave. That was why he had been picked as a government worker. He took great risks every day, pushing through the ice and snow from daylight to dark.

Perrault took his team across ice so thin that it bent. Once Dave and Buck broke through. By the time they were dragged out, they were half frozen and nearly drowned. They were coated with ice. Frank built a fire and made Dave and Buck run around it. They ran around and around, so close that their fur was burned by the flames. At last the ice melted and their fur dried.

Another time Spitz fell through the ice. He dragged the whole team after him up to Buck. But Buck pulled backward with all his might. He dug his paws into the thin ice, which snapped and shook around him. Dave stood behind Buck, pulling backward as hard as he could. Behind the sled, Frank pulled as hard as he could.

Another time, the ice broke away all around. The only way out was blocked by a steep cliff. Perrault went up the cliff. Then he made a long rope out of the harness and straps and pulled the dogs up, one after another. Next he pulled up the sled. Then he helped Frank climb up.

The men used the rope to come down again in another place. The slow, hard work took all day. By night they were back on the river. It had taken them all the day to go a part of a mile!

When the men reached the next river, their luck turned. Perrault pushed the worn-out dogs ahead, trying to make up time. In one day they made thirty-five miles to the Big Salmon River. The next day they went thirty-five more miles to the Little Salmon. The third day they left forty miles behind them. They were getting close to the Five Fingers.

Buck's feet were not as hard as the feet of other sled dogs. He limped all day in pain. The minute camp was made, he lay down. Hungry as he was, he could not get up to eat his fish. Frank had to bring it to him.

Frank knew that Buck's feet were sore. He felt sorry for him. After supper he rubbed

Buck's feet. He even made foot pads for Buck out of the tops of an old pair of boots.

One morning Frank forgot about Buck's pads. Buck lay down on his back in the snow. He waved his feet in the air and barked at Frank. Perrault watched him and smiled. Frank put the pads on Buck.

Later, when Buck became more used to the trail and his feet grew harder, Frank threw his worn pads away.

One morning, at the Pelly River, Dolly went mad. Without any warning she burst into a long wolf howl. The other dogs looked up with fear. Dolly sprang for Buck.

Buck had never before seen a dog go mad. Yet he turned and raced away. Dolly, panting and foaming at the mouth, was only one leap behind. She could not gain on him, but he could not get away from her. Buck ran on. He tore across the ice. He dared not look back. He heard Dolly snarling. Then he heard Frank call him.

Buck turned back. His lungs were almost bursting, and he gasped for air. He knew Frank would have to help him.

Frank was waiting, an axe raised in his hand. Buck shot past him, and Frank swung his axe down upon Dolly's head. She fell at his feet.

Buck got to the dog sled. He fell against it, panting for air.

Now Spitz saw his chance. He sprang upon the fallen Buck. With his sharp teeth, he ripped Buck's leg to the bone.

Frank came to save Buck. The driver's heavy whip came down upon Spitz. Buck watched him get a bad beating.

"That Spitz—he's a devil!" said Perrault. "Some day he'll kill Buck."

"That Buck—he's two devils," Frank said. "I have watched him. I know. Listen! Someday he'll get mad at Spitz. Then he will chew him up and spit him out on the snow."

From then on, it was open war between Spitz and Buck. Spitz, as lead dog, was boss of the sled team. Buck was the only dog from the south he had seen who could stand up on the northern trails. All the others had died on the trail. Buck was hard and smart. He could match Spitz in any way.

Spitz did not know that Buck knew enough to take his time. Buck knew his chance would come, and he waited for it.

As the days went by, Buck worked harder than ever. The sled team got closer and closer to Dawson. Buck now wanted to be the leader. His hate for Spitz grew. Things now began to go wrong. There was always fighting among the dogs. No one knew it, but Buck was at the bottom of the trouble.

One dark afternoon they pulled into Dawson, the end of the trail. The great fight was still to come.

CHAPTER 7

The Great Fight

At Dawson there was a great camp. Many men and dogs were at work. All day and all night, dog teams went up and down the streets. The dogs were pulling firewood and other things. They did all the hard work. Buck remembered the heavy work he had seen horses do on Judge Miller's ranch in California.

Sometimes Buck met another dog from the south. But most of the dogs he saw were wild, wolf-like huskies of the North. Every night they howled like wolves. At nine o'clock, at twelve o'clock, and again at three o'clock in the morning, they lifted their noses and howled at the sky.

Buck loved to hear them. Before long he howled with them in the call of the wild.

Buck watched the Northern Lights. They would flash and shoot halfway across the skies. This strange and beautiful sight made him restless and uneasy. The sky, wide and clear, stretched overhead as far as the eye could see. The land lay frozen under a heavy blanket of snow.

The howl of the huskies was a sad song. It was an old song.

For seven days, Perrault and Frank stayed at Dawson. Then they started back. Perrault wanted to make the fastest trip of the year.

"The papers I am taking," he said to Frank, "are very important. We must hurry!"

"Oh, we can do it," said Frank. "This dog team is the best in the North. Nobody ever saw a faster team of dogs."

"They have had a week's rest," said Perrault. "They have done nothing but eat and sleep. They are ready to go now."

"The trail is packed. Many dog sleds came after we did. We will go so fast that it will be like skating."

They started out fast. They broke a record and went sixty miles the first day. The second day they kept up their speed. But this time things were different with the dogs. The dogs were now following Buck more than Spitz.

One night Pike stole half of Spitz's food and ate it while Buck watched. Another night, Spitz tried to nip Dub and Joe for something they had done wrong. But they teamed up and beat him off.

Buck never came near Spitz without snarling and showing his teeth. Buck grew worse every day. He no longer kept out of Spitz's way. He almost dared Spitz to start something.

The dogs now began to fight more among themselves. Frank did all he could to stop them. He stamped the snow in his anger. He whipped them again and again. But as soon as his back was turned, the dogs were fighting again.

Frank backed Spitz, the leader of the team. But Buck sided against him and with the other eight dogs. Frank knew that Buck was making the trouble. But Buck was too clever to be caught. He worked hard in the harness. But he also started fights.

One night they camped at the mouth of a river. After supper Dub spotted a rabbit. It jumped out of its hiding place in the bushes and Dub went after it. In a second the whole dog team had followed.

A hundred yards away, some Northwest Mounted Police were camped. Their fifty dogs all joined Buck's team in the rabbit chase. The rabbit sped down the river. It turned off into a small frozen creek.

The sixty dogs soon fell far behind. Buck was in the lead. He ran his best. His big body went forward, leap by leap.

He wanted to kill.

Buck was happy as he led the pack. He howled the old wolf cry.

Spitz left the pack of running dogs. Without Buck's knowing it, he cut across the bend of the creek. He leaped from a bank right beside the rabbit. His sharp teeth broke the rabbit's back in one snap. The rabbit screamed. The pack of dogs howled.

Buck did not cry out. He leaped at Spitz but he missed the throat. Over and over the two dogs rolled in the snow. Spitz got to his feet. He slashed Buck's leg, leaped clear, and backed away to get better footing.

Buck knew the time had come at last. It was the death fight.

The two dogs slowly went around and around. They watched each other. Each wanted the first chance to attack.

The other dogs stood in a ring around Spitz and Buck. Their eyes shone. They waited. Buck knew just what he wanted to do.

Spitz had had many fights. He had beaten all kinds of dogs. He had never lost. Spitz never fought until he was ready.

Buck tried first to sink his teeth into Spitz's neck. Spitz beat him off. Their teeth ground together. Their lips were cut and bleeding. Buck tried, but he could not get through his enemy's guard.

Then Buck rushed Spitz again and again. Time and again he snapped at the snow-white throat. But each time Spitz slashed Buck and got away.

Then Buck tried a trick. He started to rush for Spitz's throat. Then he turned his

head and tried to throw Spitz over. But Spitz jumped lightly away, slashing Buck's shoulder.

Spitz was not cut once, but Buck was streaming with blood and panting hard. The ring of dogs watched. They crept closer. They were ready to chew up the loser.

Buck panted harder now. Spitz rushed for his throat. Buck almost went down. Spitz hit him again. Buck went over. The ring of dogs moved closer. But Buck was back on his feet. The dogs stopped moving in. They would have to wait longer.

Up to now, Buck had fought without thinking. But he could think, too. He stopped for just a second. Then he rushed at Spitz's shoulder. At the last second, he dropped low and got Spitz's left front leg between his teeth.

There was the crack of breaking bone. Spitz faced Buck on three legs. Buck did the same trick again and broke Spitz's other front leg.

Spitz fought on madly. He saw the ring of shining eyes and sharp teeth closing in on him. He had often been part of such a ring in the past. This time he was inside it.

Buck would not spare Spitz. He got ready for the last rush. He could feel the breath of the huskies at his back. He could see them, waiting for the end.

Spitz swung back and forth, snarling. Buck sprang again. His shoulder rammed Spitz's shoulder. The big white dog rolled over in the snow.

The dogs killed Spitz in a few seconds. Buck watched. He had killed his enemy. Now he was the leader.

CHAPTER 8

Buck, the Leader

"See? I told you Buck was two devils!" Frank said the next morning. Spitz was missing, and Buck was covered with blood.

"Now we'll make better time. No more Spitz, no more trouble. You will see!"

Perrault packed the camp outfit onto the sled. Frank harnessed the dogs. Buck trotted up to the leader's place where Spitz used to be. Frank led Sol-leks to the lead place, but Buck sprang upon Sol-leks, driving him back. Then Buck walked over to the lead again.

"What's this?" laughed Frank. "Look at Buck. He killed Spitz. Now he thinks he'll take Spitz's job. Go away," he cried.

Buck did not move.

Then Frank took Buck by the neck and dragged him to the side. He put Sol-leks back in the lead. Old Sol-leks was afraid of Buck. When Frank turned his back again, Buck chased Sol-leks away.

Frank was angry. He grabbed a club and started for Buck.

"I'll fix you!" he yelled.

Buck remembered the man in the red sweater. He stepped back slowly. The next time Frank brought Sol-leks into the lead place, Buck made no move.

Frank harnessed the team and tied down the load. When he was ready to put Buck back in his old place, he called to him. But Buck did not come. He stepped back. Frank followed him. Buck moved out of reach.

Thinking Buck was afraid of the club, Frank threw it down. But Buck just wanted to be the leader. He had won the place. He would take nothing less.

Perrault came to help. The men chased Buck for almost an hour. They threw clubs at him. They called him. He made no move to run away, but he stayed out of their reach.

Frank sat down on a log. He scratched his head. Perrault looked at his watch. They were losing time. Then Frank shook his head and grinned at Perrault.

"Let's give him his way," he said.

"We might as well. He will be a good leader," said Perrault.

Frank went to the head of the team. He called Buck. Buck did not come. Frank got Sol-leks and put him back in his old place. The dog team stood harnessed to the sled, ready for the trail. The only place for Buck was at the lead. Frank called again and dropped his club. Buck trotted to him. He got into the place he had won. Frank tied the lines. Then they were off.

Before the day was over, Frank found that Buck was a good leader. Frank had thought that Spitz was the best lead dog he ever saw, but now he found that Buck was even better.

Buck whipped Pike, who was lazy. Before the first day ended, Pike was doing more work than he ever had. The first night in camp Buck nipped Joe, who had made trouble, until Joe ran for help.

Buck got the team to work together. Once more the dogs leaped to the sled in the morn-

51

ing. A day or so later, Teek and Koona, two northern huskies, were added to the team. Buck broke them in quickly.

"I never saw a dog like Buck!" Frank cried to Perrault. "I never saw such a dog before. He's worth every cent you paid for him! What do you say?"

Perrault smiled and nodded. The dog team was ahead of the record now. They were gaining every day. The trail was hard and fast, and Perrault was happy. It was not too cold—only fifty below zero. The men took turns riding.

Thirty-Mile River had frozen over. In one day they made a sixty-mile run. They flew across the seventy miles of lakes. On they went for two more weeks. The end of the run was in sight!

It was a record run. For two weeks they had made forty miles a day. Perrault and Frank bragged about their fast run in the streets of Skagway. Everybody came out to look at the dog team.

New orders came from the government for Frank and Perrault. The next day they were gone. Buck never knew where they went. Like other men, they passed out of Buck's life for good.

A Scotch half-breed now took over the dog team. They started back over the Dawson Trail. About a dozen dog teams made the trip together. This time it was not light, easy running. It was hard work every day, pulling a heavy mail sled.

Buck was too tired from the work to like it. Still, he tried to do it well.

Every morning the cooks built fires and cooked breakfast. After breakfast the men broke camp and harnessed the dogs. In less than an hour they were on the trail again.

At night, when camp was made, the men put up the tents, cut firewood, brought water for cooking, and fed the dogs.

In all, there were more than a hundred dogs in the teams. There were some good fighters in the lot. Three fights showed that Buck could beat the best of them.

Buck loved to lie close to the fire. Sometimes his thoughts went back to his old life. He remembered his life at Judge Miller's ranch in California. It seemed a long time ago.

Sometimes Buck remembered the man in the red sweater. He remembered Curly's death. He remembered his fight with Spitz. He remembered good things he had eaten. But he was not homesick. He knew the past would never come back.

Buck sometimes dreamed as he slept by the fire. Strange thoughts would make the hair rise along his back. He cried or growled in his sleep.

"Hey, you, Buck, wake up!" the cook would shout.

And Buck would get up and stretch.

It was a hard trip. The dogs lost weight and got weaker. When they reached Dawson, the end of the trail, they were worn out. They should have rested for at least a week.

But in just two days the team started on the trip back to Skagway. This time they were loaded with mail going out. It snowed every day, and the trail was soft. It was harder for the dogs to pull the sled. The drivers did their best to be fair to the dogs.

Each night the dogs got good care. They ate before the men did. No man went to his bed without looking over the feet of his dogs. Still the dogs became weaker. Even the strongest dogs were showing the strain. They had gone 1800 miles!

Billy cried in his sleep every night. Joe was meaner than ever. No one could get near Sol-leks. Even Buck was very, very tired.

Dave was the worst of all. Something was wrong with him. As soon as camp was made, he lay down where he had eaten. He did not get up until morning.

Sometimes, in the harness, Dave cried out with pain. His driver could find nothing wrong. All the other drivers wondered what the trouble was.

One night after supper the men carried Dave to the fires. They felt his body and legs. He cried out many times. Something was wrong inside him.

In a few days, Dave was so weak that he fell many times on the trail. The driver of his sled stopped. He thought Dave should rest. He wanted to let him run along behind the sled. But Dave did not want to be taken out of the harness. He cried when he saw Sol-leks moved into the place he had held so long. He was sick, but he did not want another dog to do his work.

The sled started up again. Dave ran along, biting Sol-leks and trying to push him away.

The driver chased him off with the whip. Dave would not run along behind the sled. He fell down in the snow. As the long train of dogsleds went on, he howled with pain.

Soon Dave was far behind the sled. When the train stopped, he caught up. He found his own sled, went to it, and stood beside Sol-leks.

The driver was lighting his pipe. He watched Dave for a minute. Then the sleds started again. But Dave's sled did not move. The driver came to check. Dave had bitten through Sol-leks harness! He stood in front of the sled in his own place.

"A good dog's heart will break if you take him out of the harness," said another driver.

"But the work is killing him," said Dave's driver. "He can't stand it."

Then a third man came over.

"I have seen it many times," he said. "A dog wants to die in the harness."

"Don't cut him out of the harness," said another. "It's better to let him die there."

So Dave was put in his old place again. He pulled proudly. Again he cried out in pain. Many times he fell down and was dragged in the harness. Once the sled ran into him.

But he held out. That night the driver made a place for him by the fire. By morning Dave was too weak to move. He tried to crawl to the driver. Then he tried to get to his feet. But he fell in the snow.

It was time to start. Dave's sled team moved away with the others, leaving him behind. They could hear Dave howling.

The sleds stopped. Dave's driver slowly walked back on the trail. In a few minutes, a shot rang out.

The driver ran back to the sled. Whips snapped. Bells rang. The sleds moved on.

But Buck and every other dog knew what had happened behind them on the trail.

CHAPTER 9

The Work
on the Trail

For almost five months the dog team dragged the sled back and forth to Dawson. Buck and his teammates were worn out.

In less than five months they had gone 2500 miles. They had made four round trips over the Dawson Trail. During the last 1800 miles, they had had only five days' rest. When they dragged into Skagway, they could hardly move the sled.

"Mush on, poor sore feet," said the driver of Buck's team to the dogs. "This is the last stop. Now we get a long rest, a good, long rest!"

The thin, foot-sore dogs limped down the main street of Skagway.

The drivers of all the teams really thought that they had a long rest coming. They needed it, and so did the dogs. But big loads of mail and orders were waiting for them. A few fresh dogs were there. They were to take the place of some of the dogs worn down by the trail.

Three days later, Buck and his mates were just beginning to get some rest. But, on the morning of the fourth day, two men bought the sled, the harness, and the dogs.

Buck saw the men talking and pointing to the dogs. He saw the money being paid. Buck knew that these drivers were now passing out of his life. Other men had passed out of his life before. He did not like the looks of Hal and Charles, the new owners.

Charles was a middle-aged man with weak eyes and pale skin. Hal was a young man of about nineteen. He carried a gun and a hunting knife strapped around his waist. Both men were out of place in this wild land. They should never have come to Alaska.

Hal and Charles took the dog team to their camp. The tent was put up wrong. The dishes were not washed.

Mercedes, Charles's wife and Hal's sister, waited for them.

Buck watched the men take down the tent and load the sled. They didn't know what they were doing. They made the tent roll three times too big. They packed away their dishes without washing them. Mercedes scolded and got in the way. The sled was packed, unpacked, and packed again.

Three men stopped to watch.

"You've got a big load without your tent," one said. "I wouldn't take it."

"How would I get along without a tent?" cried Mercedes.

"It won't be cold any more," said the man. "It's spring now."

"Your load is top-heavy," said another man. "How do you think your dogs can pull such a badly packed sled?"

"That's easy," said Hal. "I'll show you."

He took the gee-pole in one hand. He swung the whip with the other.

"Mush!" he shouted to the dog team. "Mush on there!"

The dogs, tired as they were, began to pull. They tried hard for a few minutes. Then they stopped. They could not move the sled.

"The lazy brutes! I'll show them!" Hal cried, raising the whip.

"Oh, Hal!" cried Mercedes, running to grab his arm. "You mustn't whip the dogs! The poor dears! If you're going to whip them, I won't go another step!"

"Let me alone!" yelled her brother. "They're lazy! You've got to whip them to make them work. Ask any of those men."

"The trouble is that the dogs are tired out. They need a good, long rest," said one of the men.

"Never mind him," Mercedes said to her brother. "You know better than he does!"

Hal's whip fell on the dogs. Again they tried to move the sled. They dug their feet into the packed snow. Leaning down low, they gave all they had. But the sled held. Hal's whip landed on the dogs' backs.

"Why don't you break the sled loose?" said one of the men who were watching. "It's frozen fast in the ice."

Hal tried once again to drive the dogs with the whip. This time he pushed against the gee-pole, moving it right and left. A little of this, and the sled broke loose. Overloaded and top-heavy, the sled moved slowly ahead. Hal whipped the dogs harder.

A hundred yards ahead, the path turned down a hill into the main street of Skagway. Any good driver could have kept the sled from turning over. Hal swung on the turn, and the sled fell over. Half the load spilled out on the street.

The dogs did not stop. They dragged the empty sled on its side behind them. Buck was very angry. He ran. The team followed his lead. Away they went!

"Stop! Stop!" yelled Hal, chasing them.

He slipped on the ice and fell. The dogs ran on. All along the streets the men laughed.

A few men stopped the dogs and picked up the load from the snow.

"Half the load and twice the dogs," said one man, "if you ever want to reach Dawson."

"Throw away all those canned goods," said another.

"You've got twice as many blankets as you need."

"Throw away that tent!"

"Those dishes!" said an old man. "Get rid of them! Do you think you're going by train?"

Mercedes cried, but the load was cut in half. It was still too big. Hal and Charles got more dogs. The team now had fourteen dogs, but Buck saw that the new ones were not trained and not fit for such hard work. He could teach them what not to do. He could not teach them what to do.

One sled could not carry the food needed for fourteen dogs. Charles and Hal did not know this.

Late the next morning, Buck led the long team up the street. The dogs were dead tired. Buck knew that he was starting the long, hard trip again. His heart was not in the work. The new dogs were afraid. The old dogs did not like Hal and Charles.

The new owners had learned nothing about camping. It took them half the night to set up camp. It took them half the morning to break camp. The sled was so badly loaded that during the day they had to stop and load it again. Some days they went only ten miles, and some days they didn't get started at all.

Before long, Hal and Charles ran short on dog food. They had too many dogs. They fed the dogs too much.

But it was not food that Buck and the others needed. It was rest. They were making poor time. The heavy load wore them down.

One day Hal saw that his dog food was half gone. They were less than halfway to Dawson. Hal cut down on the dog food. He tried to drive the dogs faster to cover more ground.

Dub was the first to die. It was true that he was not a bright dog and was often caught stealing. But Dub was a good worker. His sore shoulder was not treated, nor could he rest. He grew weaker each day. At last Hal shot him.

A dog of the North can get along on less food than can a dog from the southland. The six new dogs starved to death, one after another.

Mercedes and the two men snapped at one another. They simply were not fit for the hard life of the North. They fought among themselves and didn't take care of the dogs and the camp.

Mercedes wanted the men to take care of her. Sore and tired, she wanted to ride on the sled. Her extra one hundred twenty pounds made the load too heavy. The weak, starving dogs could not pull the extra load. The sled stood still. Charles and Hal begged her to walk, but she would not.

Once they lifted her from the sled. She sat down on the trail. The sled went on, and she sat there without moving. After they had gone three miles, Charles and Hal unloaded the sled and took it back to get Mercedes.

None of them cared about the dogs.

A few days later the dog food gave out. An old squaw traded them a few pounds of frozen horsehide for Hal's gun. This horsehide was poor food. It was hard as wood. The hair on it made the dogs sick.

All this time, Buck led the poor, starving team. He pulled when he could. When he could no longer pull, he fell. He stayed down until Hal whipped or clubbed him to his feet.

His coat was matted with blood. His body was thin. His ribs showed through his loose hide. He was a sorry-looking dog. But Buck would not give up.

Buck's teammates also were walking bags of bones. The seven dogs, beaten, clubbed, and starved, seemed to be seven ghost dogs. When the sled stopped, they dropped in their tracks. When the whip hit them, they got slowly to their feet.

One day gentle Billy fell and could not get up. Hal hit him on the head with an ax. Then he cut his body out of the harness and dragged it to the side of the trail.

Koona died the next day. Now only five dogs were left. Joe was too tired to be cross. Pike was limping badly. One-eyed Sol-leks, still trying, was very weak. Teek and Buck were almost blind. Buck kept the trail by feeling it with his feet.

CHAPTER 10

Buck Fails

Spring is a beautiful time in Alaska. The days grow longer. Dawn breaks by three in the morning. The light stays until nine at night. The long day is full of sunshine. Life awakens all over the land.

Crickets sing at night, and birds sing in the daytime. Squirrels chatter in the trees. The wild birds come from the south and honk overhead. The great Yukon River begins to break loose from the ice that holds it.

Spring burst upon them, but the dog sled crawled slowly on. Finally Hal, Charles, and Mercedes staggered into John Thornton's camp. There they stopped, and the dogs dropped as if dead.

John Thornton was cutting an ax handle from a branch. He listened to Hal's story. He knew the two men were fools . . . he had seen many such fools before.

"Don't take any more chances on the rotten ice," Thornton warned them. "Don't cross White River. You'll never make it."

"They told us we couldn't make it this far. But here we are!" said Hal.

"And they told you the truth," John Thornton answered. "The ice will go any moment. You have had fool's luck. I wouldn't cross White River on the ice for all the gold in Alaska!"

"All the same, we're going on to Dawson!" said Hal. "Get up there, Buck! Mush on!"

Thornton went on cutting. It was useless to talk to a fool.

The dog team did not get up when Hal called. He beat them with his whip. John Thornton bit his lips to keep from saying anything.

First Sol-leks made it to his feet. Teek was next. Then Joe came up crying with pain. Pike tried and tried and then got to his feet. Buck did not try. He lay where he had fallen. The whip bit into him time after time.

Thornton watched Hal whip Buck. He stood up and walked up and down.

Hal screamed at Buck. It was the first time Buck had failed. Hal threw down the whip and used a club. Buck had made up his mind not to get up. He had known all day that the rotten ice was not safe. He would not move.

Buck was so nearly dead that the blows did not hurt him much. He could hear the club hit his body. But he could not feel it. It seemed very far away.

John Thornton could stand no more. He sprang upon Hal and hit him. Hal fell. Mercedes screamed.

John Thornton went over to Buck.

"If you hit that dog again, I'll kill you!" he said at last to Hal.

"It's my dog," Hal said. "Get out of my way."

Thornton stood between Hal and Buck. He would not get out of the way. Hal got out his hunting knife. Thornton took the ax handle he was making and hit Hal's fist with it. The knife fell to the ground. Hal reached for it, but Thornton hit his hand again with the ax handle. Then Thornton stooped over and picked up the knife himself. With two strokes he cut Buck's harness.

A few minutes later, Buck raised his head. He saw the sled pull away from Thornton's camp with Pike leading and Sol-leks at the wheel. Between were Joe and Teek. Mercedes rode the loaded sled.

Thornton sat down beside Buck. With a kind hand, he felt for broken bones. He watched the sled crawl over the ice of the White River, a quarter of a mile away.

With a crash, it broke through the weak ice. The gee-pole, with Hal hanging to it, sailed into the air. Mercedes screamed. Charles turned and started back. A big patch of ice gave way. Dogs and people were gone. There was only a big, black hole in the ice.

John Thornton and Buck looked at each other.

"You poor devil," said John Thornton.

Buck licked his hand.

CHAPTER 11

For the Love
of a Man

When John Thornton's feet had frozen on the trail, his partners had made him a good place to stay and had gone on. Thornton still limped a little when Buck first saw him. In the warm sun his feet got much better. Soon he did not limp at all.

Buck stayed around camp with Thornton. Through the warm spring day Buck rested near the riverbank. He watched the water running by, listened to the songs of the birds overhead, and slowly grew stronger.

After three thousand miles of the hardest kind of work, it was good to rest. Buck's wounds healed. Soon his thin ribs were covered again.

Thornton camped beside White River and waited for his partners to come back on a

raft. He planned to go with them to Dawson. Day after day, Thornton, his two dogs, and Buck loafed and waited.

Skeet was Thornton's little Irish setter. She first made friends with Buck when he was too weak to care. As a mother cat washes her kittens, Skeet washed Buck's wounds. She came to him and licked his wounds. Buck began to watch for her.

Nig was a big black dog, half bloodhound and half deerhound. This happy dog was also friendly to Buck.

Skeet and Nig liked Buck, and Buck liked them. It seemed that John Thornton had enough love for all three dogs, and they all enjoyed his love. When Buck grew stronger, the three dogs romped and played games. Even Thornton joined in the fun. Buck had found a new life, a happy one.

Deep and real love now came to Buck for the first time. At Judge Miller's ranch in California, it had been different. The Judge had been a kind friend. Buck had liked him. He had enjoyed caring for the Miller boys. But he had never loved anyone the way he did John Thornton. He loved the man deeply, almost madly.

John Thornton had saved his life. That was one reason for Buck to love him. But Thornton was also a kind and good master. He looked after his dogs as if they were his own children. He talked to them kindly. Sometimes he just sat down to "gas" with them, as he called it. He enjoyed this as much as they did.

Sometimes the man took Buck's head in his hands. Then he put his head down on Buck's. Sometimes he shook the dog back and forth and called him names. Buck knew no greater joy than to have Thornton do this. When Thornton shook him, he felt as if his heart would jump out of his body.

When Thornton let him go, Buck would leap to his feet, pull back his lips, and grin. Deep sounds came from his throat. He looked at Thornton, his heart bursting with love.

"You can almost speak!" cried Thornton.

Buck had a strange way of showing love. Grabbing Thornton's hand in his mouth, he would close his jaws so hard that Thornton's skin showed the toothmarks. Thornton knew that this bite meant love. And Buck knew, when Thornton shook him and called him names, that this, too, was love.

Buck loved Thornton, but he did not beg for all of Thornton's time. He was happy to love him from afar. He stayed at Thornton's feet for hours, watching the man's face. When he lay farther away, their eyes sometimes met. Without any words, both the man and the dog knew that they had deep love between them.

For a long time, Buck would not let Thornton go away from him. He followed everywhere at the man's heels. His other masters had all left him. He was afraid that Thornton, too, might leave him.

Sometimes at night Buck dreamed about this. Waking up, he would walk over to Thornton's tent, where the man was sleeping. When he heard Thornton breathe and knew he was still there, he felt better.

In some ways his love for John Thornton had made Buck gentle. In other ways he was still wild.

Buck stole from nearby camps and was so clever that he was never caught. He never stole from John Thornton.

Nor did Buck fight with Skeet and Nig, for they belonged to his beloved master. Buck did fight any strange dog. He had learned from Spitz and other strong fighters that he must kill or be killed. There was no other way. Buck knew he must live by the law of the North, and show no mercy.

Buck sat dreaming by John Thornton's fire in the evenings with his nose on his paws. But Buck's wild blood—the blood of his wolf fathers—called to him. Each day the things he had learned in peaceful California slipped a little farther away. Soon he could not remember when he had not been a dog of the North.

A call sounded deep in the forest. When Buck heard it, he wanted to turn his back on the fire and to run away, deep into the woods.

Once or twice he started into the forest to answer this call of the wild. But the love of John Thornton drew him back. Thornton alone held him. Only his love for this man kept Buck from becoming a wild dog.

One day Thornton's partners came on their raft. Hans and Pete, like Thornton, were brave men of the North. Like Thornton they lived hard lives. Buck could see at once that they were good men and good friends.

Buck's love for John Thornton grew and grew. He would do anything for his beloved master.

"It's a terrible thing," said Thornton one day, "to think how that dog loves me. Sometimes it makes me afraid."

"I wouldn't want to be the man to lay a hand on you while Buck was around," said Pete.

"By jingo, I wouldn't either!" said Hans.

Before many weeks, Buck showed what he would do to a man who tried to harm Thornton. They were at a gold-mining town farther north.

Black Burton was there that night. He was a man with a bad name. He had been picking a fight with someone. Thornton stepped between the two men to stop the fight. Buck

was lying over in a corner watching his master. He had his eyes on every move of Black Burton's.

Suddenly Burton hit Thornton with his fist. Thornton grabbed at a table to keep from falling over.

Then Buck made one long leap through the air. He gave a deep roar. The one jump carried him to Burton's throat. Burton threw up his arm to save his life. Buck dashed him to the floor and jumped on top of him, driving with his teeth for the man's throat. Burton fought and kept him away.

As it was, Burton's throat was bleeding before the crowd fell upon Buck and pulled him away. While a doctor tended Burton's wounds, Buck walked up and down, growling. Men with clubs held him back.

Later the men talked things over. Buck was right, they said, in helping his master. No one blamed him for trying to save Thornton.

From that day on, Buck was talked about all over Alaska because he was so brave and loyal.

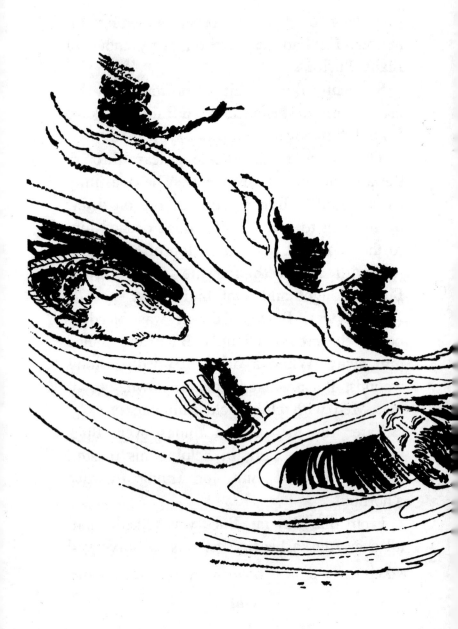

CHAPTER 12

Buck Saves
John Thornton

Later that fall, Buck saved Thornton's life. Hans, Pete, and Thornton were taking a boat down a creek that had become a rushing river. At one place there was a very bad stretch of rushing water. Hans and Pete were on the bank. They held ropes tied at one end of the boat and moved slowly up the creek.

Thornton was in the boat, pushing with a pole. It was his job to keep the boat from turning over. Buck was on the bank. He ran along, keeping up with the boat, never taking his eyes off his master.

At last they came to a very bad spot where they had to take the boat around some sharp rocks in the river. The boat went over and Thornton fell into the roaring stream. The water carried him downstream toward some sharp rocks. No swimmer could live in that wild stretch of water.

When he saw Thornton fall, Buck sprang into the river. Swimming strongly, he soon reached his master. When he felt Thornton grab his tail, Buck turned and started for the riverbank. Buck was a powerful swimmer, but he was carried downstream. He could not reach the shore in the strong current.

From below came the awful roar of rapids. There the wild river dropped and rushed over big rocks. The current pulled everything into the rapids. Thornton knew they could not make the shore. He felt himself hit the first of the rocks. Then he hit a big rock. Letting go of Buck's tail, he hung on to the slippery rock with both hands.

"Go, Buck! Go!" he shouted.

Buck was swept on downstream, fighting hard. Throwing himself partly out of the water, he turned to look back at Thornton. Then he swam as hard as he could toward the bank. A little farther on, Pete and Hans dragged him ashore.

No man could hang on to a slippery rock for long in that wild river. Hans and Pete ran back to where they had left the boat. They tied a long rope to Buck's shoulders. Then they put him once more into the stream.

Swimming hard, Buck headed out for Thornton. But the rushing water swept him past the rock where Thornton was hanging. Hans and Pete saw what had happened. As hard as they could, they pulled on the rope, bringing Buck back again. In the strong current, Buck was swept under the water. When they got Buck back to the shore, he was almost drowned.

The two men threw themselves upon Buck. They pounded the water out of his lungs, and he started to breathe again. Buck got to his feet and fell again. Then he heard Thornton calling him from the rock in the river.

Thornton's voice brought Buck to his feet. He dashed up the bank ahead of the men, to the place where he had jumped in the last time.

Again Hans and Pete tied the rope around his chest. Again Buck struck out swimming, with Hans and Pete holding the rope. This time he would not miss. Buck headed for the water above Thornton. Then he headed downstream for his master.

Thornton saw Buck coming. Reaching up with both arms, he hugged the big dog's neck. Hans tied the rope around a tree on the bank. Then he and Pete began pulling. Buck and Thornton were pulled under by the rushing water. Fighting together, the man and the dog were dragged toward shore. They were beaten against the rocks and choked by the water.

Hans and Pete pulled them to the shore. They rolled Thornton face down over a log until he came to his senses. As soon as he opened his eyes, he thought of Buck. He looked around to see where the dog was. Buck lay limp in the grass. Nig, sitting close by, was howling. Skeet was licking Buck's wet face and closed eyes.

Thornton dragged himself to where Buck lay. In a few moments Buck began to move.

Thornton felt carefully all over the dog's body. He found three broken ribs.

"That ends it!" Thornton said to Hans and Pete. "We camp right here!"

On that spot the three men set up camp. There they stayed until Buck's broken ribs got better and he was able to go on again.

CHAPTER 13

"What a Dog, Sir!"

They spent that winter in Dawson, and Buck won fame again—this time in a different way. This time he won a lot of money for the three partners. With the money they were able to buy a new outfit and go look for gold. This was how it happened.

One day in Dawson, some men were bragging about their dogs. Thornton was one of them. One man said his dog could start a sled loaded with five hundred pounds and walk off with it. Another man said his dog could carry six hundred pounds. A third man said that his dog could pull seven hundred.

"Pooh!" said John Thornton. "Buck can start a thousand pounds!"

"And break it out?" asked the third man, called Matt. "And walk off with it for a hundred yards?"

"That's right!" said Thornton. "He can break it out. And he can walk off with it for a hundred yards."

"Well," said Matt, turning to the men in the crowd standing around. "I'll bet a thousand dollars he can't! And here is my money!"

From his pocket he took a sack of gold dust and laid it on the table. Nobody spoke.

Now it was up to Thornton to prove his claim for Buck. Thornton, to tell the truth, did not know if Buck could start a thousand pounds. Half a ton! Had he gone too far with his boasting? He had often wondered if Buck could start half a ton. But he did not know, for he had never tried it.

The eyes of a dozen men were on Thornton. He sat there waiting and thinking. A thousand dollars? He had no thousand dollars, nor did Hans and Pete.

"Losing your nerve?" asked Matt, patting his sack of gold. "I've got a sled outside now. It has twenty fifty-pound sacks of flour on it. What are we waiting for?"

Thornton did not answer. He did not know what to say. He looked from one man to another. Then, in the ring of men standing around, he saw a man he knew.

"Can you lend me a thousand dollars?" he asked.

"Sure!" said his friend. "But I don't think your dog can do the job."

Thornton's friend laid another sack of gold on the table beside the first.

All the men went out into the street. They wanted to see the test. Since it was very cold, they wore fur coats, caps, and mittens. Stamping their heavy boots, they tried to keep warm.

Matt's sled, loaded with flour, had been standing in the street for hours. It was sixty below zero, and the sled runners had frozen fast to the hard-packed snow.

All around men began to make bets. Some men said that Thornton had a right to knock the sled runners loose from the ice. Then Buck would have to break out the sled from a standstill. But Matt said no. Buck, he said, had to break the sled runners from the frozen snow. Most of the men said he was right. Not one man believed Buck could do that.

Thornton himself was almost sure he would lose the bet. He wished he had not been so foolish in the first place. Ten dogs, he saw, were hitched to Matt's sled. How could Buck do the work of ten good dogs?

"Everybody is betting against Buck," said Matt. "Nobody thinks he can win. The bets are three to one against him. I'll bet you another thousand, three to one."

Thornton called Hans and Pete to him. They talked together for a minute. Between them, the two men had only two hundred dollars. Yet they gladly gave it to John Thornton to bet against Matt's six hundred dollars, three to one.

Then the team of ten sled dogs was unhitched. Buck, in his own harness, was put before the sled. He seemed to know that something important was happening. He felt that in some way he must do something great for John Thornton.

"A fine-looking dog, that Buck!" one man said. "There's not a finer one in all Alaska!"

"He looks good," said another. "Not a bit of fat. He looks strong and fit."

Buck's furry coat shone like silk. His chest and front legs were big, but so was the rest of his body. Men felt the muscles which showed under his fur.

"His muscles are like iron," said one man, feeling Buck's shoulders. "I'll give you eight hundred dollars for him, Thornton!"

Thornton shook his head. He stepped to Buck's side.

"Stand back!" cried one man. "You must stand back. Give him room, and don't touch him!"

The crowd of men grew still. Everyone could see that Buck was a fine dog indeed. But still no one believed that he could move the thousand pounds of flour.

Then Thornton got down beside Buck. Taking the dog's great head in his two hands, he rested his own cheek on Buck's. This time he did not shake Buck's head. He just said in Buck's ear: "As you love me, Buck! As you love me!"

Buck could hardly wait to start.

The crowd of men watched Thornton rise to his feet. Buck took Thornton's mittened

hand between his teeth. He held it for just a minute. It was Buck's answer of love. Then Thornton stepped back to give Buck room.

"Now, Buck!" Thornton said.

Buck first pulled the lines tight. Then he loosened them for an inch or two. It was the way he had learned to start.

"Gee!" Thornton called.

Buck swung to the right, then ahead. The load shook and the runners cracked in the ice.

"Haw!" called Thornton to his dog.

This time Buck swung to the left. And this time the sled runners broke loose from the ice. Men could not believe what they saw.

"Now—MUSH!" cried Thornton.

Buck threw himself forward. His great chest was almost on the ground. His muscles were straining. His feet were clawing at the ice and snow.

The sled moved a bit and stopped. It almost started forward again. Buck's foot slipped. Then the sled did go ahead. One inch. Two inches. The sled jerked slowly along. Then it began to gain speed. Then it moved onward swiftly.

Thornton was running along behind Buck, talking happily to his dog. As Buck came near the end of the hundred yards, already marked off, all the men began to cheer. Then the cheer changed to a roar. Every man threw his cap and mittens into the air. Beating each other on the backs, they shook hands. The crowd was happy to see such a wonderful show of strength by a fine dog.

Thornton fell on his knees beside Buck. The man's head and the dog's head were close. His arms were around the dog's neck.

"What a dog, sir!" shouted one man, stepping out of the crowd. "I'll give you a thousand dollars for him. No, I'll make it twelve hundred. How about it?"

Thornton rose to his feet. His eyes were wet. Tears streamed down his cheeks. Buck took Thornton's hand in his teeth. Thornton reached over and shook the dog back and forth.

"Sir," said Thornton to the man who had spoken, "I'll never sell this dog!"

CHAPTER 14

Buck Hears
the Call of the Wild

Buck had made sixteen hundred dollars for John Thornton in five minutes. Now Thornton and his two friends, Hans and Pete, could look for the lost gold mine, as they wanted to.

Many stories were told about this famous lost mine. Many men had tried to find it. A few men even claimed to have seen it.

The stories about the lost mine were much the same. Some men had seen large nuggets of gold which, they claimed, came from the lost mine.

No living man had any gold from the mine to show. But the stories were never forgotten. Many men had died trying to find the mine. No one had come back with gold.

John Thornton, Pete, and Hans were now starting out to find the mine. It took time to get together enough food and other things they needed for the trip.

At last they started out. Buck, Skeet, Nig, and half a dozen other dogs were in the party. Turning east, they took a little-used trail. Other good men and dogs had failed. Would these three men do what others had not done?

They went seventy miles up the Yukon River on sleds. Then they swung to the left onto another river. They went on until the river was only a little stream. Higher and higher they climbed, into the hills and mountains.

John Thornton was not afraid of the strange, wild land. With a little salt and a gun, he could get by as long as he needed to. He was in no hurry. Like an Indian, he hunted his dinner each day in the forest. Like an Indian, if he failed to find game, he kept on anyhow. He knew he would eat sooner or later.

On this trip to the lost gold mine, the men planned to shoot game and to eat only meat. The sled carried mostly tools and gun shells.

To Buck the trip was fun. He loved the hunting, fishing, and poking into strange new places.

For weeks they went on, day after day. Then they would camp for weeks in the woods. The dogs loafed and rested. The men built big fires and made holes in the frozen ground so they could dig for gold in the gravel. Beside the campfire they washed pans of dirt, looking for gold.

Sometimes they all went hungry. Sometimes, when they found a lot of game, they ate like kings. When summer came, they built boats and went up and down strange rivers. They were deep in the Alaskan wilds.

Months came and went. Farther and deeper they went into the wild Northland. No map could show where they were. They were sure no man had ever been there before. And the lost mine—if there really was such a place—where could it be?

They crossed unknown mountains in summer snowstorms. They climbed mountains to the tops, above the timber line. They reached the deep snows on the peaks.

They went down into valleys where clouds of bugs and flies attacked them. Beside the ice and snow, they found wild strawberries. They saw mountain sides covered with wild flowers of all colors.

In the fall of that year, they came to a strange country where there were many lakes. It was a sad and silent land. They saw no life of any kind. The cold wind blew without stopping, and waves washed the lonely beaches.

The men and their dogs traveled on through another winter. Sometimes they found the trails of men who had been there long before. Once they came upon an old path. Could it lead to the Lost Cabin Mine? Where did the path come from? Where did it go? It was a strange path. It seemed to begin nowhere, and to end nowhere.

Once they came to an old hunting hut and they poked around in it. John Thornton found a long-barreled flintlock gun. This gun, he knew, had been made many, many years ago. What hunter, trapper, or miner had lost it?

Another spring came. The men still had not found the Lost Cabin Mine. They did find a stream where the gold showed like yellow butter on the bottom of the washing pan. They looked no farther.

Each day, in this spot, they panned thousands of dollars in gold dust and nuggets. They worked hard. They sacked the gold in moosehide bags. Each sack held fifty pounds of the yellow gold. When these fifty-pound bags were full, they stacked them outside the cabin like firewood.

The three friends worked like beavers. Weeks stretched into months. The yellow gold piled up and up and up.

There was little for the dogs to do. Sometimes Thornton hunted for game. The dogs carried it home. Most of the time, Buck lay dreaming by the fire. This life in the wild was the life he loved most of all. He knew he belonged here. He became part of the wild land around him.

From the deep forest, Buck again heard the call of the wild. He wanted something. What strange thing did he want? Lying there beside the fire, he did not know. What made him uneasy and restless?

Sometimes he went into the woods alone. Barking softly, he listened for an answering call. He poked his nose into the cool ground. He snorted with joy at its smell. He sometimes hid for hours behind a fallen tree. With eyes and ears wide open, he saw and heard everything about him.

Buck could not understand the call of the wild. He only heard it. Maybe he tried to find it. But he did not know what he was looking for. He knew that the call of the wild came to him again and again.

He raced down dry stream beds. Sometimes he jumped over fallen trees. He crept up and spied upon the birds.

Best of all, Buck loved the midnight sun. In the dim light, he listened to the sounds of the sleepy forest. He listened and waited for the call to come to him.

CHAPTER 15

Buck Answers the Call of the Wild

One night Buck leaped from his sleep. He could plainly hear the call of the wild. It was a long howl, like nothing else he had ever heard.

Buck ran through the sleeping camp. Silently, swiftly, he dashed into the woods. As he came closer to the cry, he went slower and more carefully. He came to an open place among the trees. Sitting there, nose pointed to the dim sky, was a long, lean timber wolf.

Buck had made no noise, but the wolf stopped howling and listened. Buck walked into the open, ready to be friends or ready to fight.

The wolf ran when he saw Buck. Buck followed, wild to overtake the timber wolf. He chased the wolf into the bed of a stream. Some fallen logs blocked the way. Then the wolf turned on his hind legs. Buck remembered Joe, the cornered husky. This was what he had done. The wolf snarled and showed his teeth.

Buck did not attack. He walked around the wolf slowly. The wolf was afraid, for Buck was three times as big as he was. Watching for his chance, the wolf darted away, with Buck after him again.

Time and again, Buck overtook the wolf. But Buck did not try to fight. At last the wolf understood that the big dog meant no harm. They sniffed noses. Then they became friendly. They began to play. Both were fighters, but they wanted to be friends.

At last the wolf started to run away. He made it plain to Buck that he was to come also. Side by side they ran through the darkness. Up the creek bed they went and up the mountain.

On the other side of the mountain they came to flat land and woods. Buck and the timber wolf ran, hour after hour, for many days. Buck was wildly happy.

At last Buck was answering the call of the wild, and he knew it. He was running by the side of his brother of the forest. He was running free in the open air.

They stopped by a running stream for a drink. Suddenly Buck remembered John Thornton. He sat down. It was strange that he had forgotten Thornton for so long a time. Looking at Buck with surprise, the wolf ran a few steps. Then he turned and came back, sniffing Buck's nose. He wanted Buck to follow again.

But Buck turned around and started slowly back. For almost an hour, the wolf ran beside him. Crying softly, he seemed to beg Buck not to go back to the camp. Then the wild wolf sat down, pointed his nose upward, and howled. It was a sad howl, and Buck heard it. But he kept on his way. The sound of the howl grew weaker until it died away.

John Thornton was eating his dinner when Buck ran into camp and sprang upon him. Buck knocked the man down and jumped upon him, licking his face. Then he took Thornton's hand in his jaws, as he used to.

"You old fool!" Thornton said into Buck's ear. "Where have you been all this time?

Why are you so glad to get back?"

Thornton shook Buck's big head back and forth in his hands. Buck was overjoyed to see his master again. For two days and nights he stayed in camp. He would not let Thornton get ten feet away. Buck followed Thornton as he worked. He watched the man while he ate. He watched him get into his bed at night. He slept beside him and watched him get up in the morning.

After two days, the call from the forest came again. This time it was plainer than before. Buck grew restless, thinking about his wild brother. He remembered the land beyond the mountain. He wanted to run with the wild wolf through the forests.

Once again Buck took to slipping off into the woods. Through the long hours he watched and listened. But he did not hear the wolf howl again. The wild brother came no more.

Now Buck began to sleep out in the forest at night. For days at a time he would stay away from camp. Once he crossed the mountain and went down into the land beyond.

He stayed for a week. He killed his food each day, and he looked for his wild brother.

He fished for salmon in a mountain stream. One day he killed a big black bear. It was a hard fight for Buck. Two days later, he came back to his kill. A dozen wolverines were fighting over the body. Buck chased them. Ten got away, but Buck killed two.

Living only on fresh meat now, Buck grew even stronger. When Thornton ran his hand over Buck's back, each hair snapped and crackled. He was quicker than ever. His muscles were like steel springs. It seemed that he would burst with life, health, and joy.

"There never was such a dog as Buck!" said John Thornton one day, as the three partners together watched Buck trot out of camp.

"I think so myself," Hans said. "He's the finest dog in the world!"

The three men did not see the terrible change in Buck as soon as he was deep in the forest. At once he became a dog of the wild. Like a shadow he stole along among the trees.

He knew how to hide. He knew how to slip up on a bird, a rabbit, or a chipmunk. He could fish in the pools and lakes. The darting fish were not too quick for him. Neither were the beavers too sly and careful. He killed only to eat, but he wanted to eat only what he killed.

As fall came on, the moose moved down from the mountain tops. Buck had already dragged down a half-grown calf that strayed away from its mother. He liked the moose meat and wanted more. One day he came upon a band of twenty, headed by a big bull moose. Standing over six feet tall, the bull was as dangerous an enemy as Buck had ever faced.

Back and forth the wild bull shook his big antlers. They were seven feet from tip to tip. His little eyes burned with a mean light. When he saw Buck, he roared angrily.

Buck headed for the bull and cut him out of the herd. It was not easy to do. He barked and danced about in front of the bull, just out of reach. The great antlers and the strong legs could have killed Buck in one blow.

The bull could not get rid of Buck. He charged Buck time after time. But Buck always jumped back. In this way, Buck got the old bull to move away from the rest of the herd.

Just as Buck had cut the old bull off from the herd, two or three of the younger bulls attacked Buck. The old bull ran to the herd again. But Buck had learned the lesson of sticking with a job. He did not give up. He stayed with the herd, slowing its march down the mountain side. He teased the young bulls and nipped the cows and the half-grown calves. He drove the old bull almost mad with anger.

For half a day this went on. Then Buck worked faster. He seemed to attack from all sides at once as he raced around the herd.

At last, as the sun dropped lower in the sky, the young bulls got tired of helping the old leader. In the twilight Buck leaped before the nose of the giant old bull.

The old bull weighed thirteen hundred pounds. He had lived a long life in the wildest part of Alaska. Fighting and killing were his life. Now he faced death in the teeth of a dog no higher than his knees.

From then on, night and day, Buck never left the old bull. He never gave him any rest. He never let him eat. He never let him drink.

Often the old bull would break away and run. But Buck would follow easily at the bull's heels. He could play the game, and in the end he would wear out the old giant. While the moose stood still, Buck would lie down and rest. When he tried to eat or drink, Buck would attack him.

The old bull grew weaker. Buck found more time to rest. At the end of the fourth day, Buck pulled the great moose down. For a day and a night he stayed by the kill. He ate and slept, slept and ate.

Then he was rested, strong, and fresh. He turned back toward camp and John Thornton.

Hour after hour he went on, running easily. Always knowing the way, he went home through the strange land.

As he drew nearer home, he began to sense that something had gone wrong. The birds and squirrels were making too much noise. The wind seemed to tell him something. When Buck reached the last part of his long run, he became very careful. Then, three miles away from camp, he came upon a strange, fresh trail that made his hair stand on end. That strange, fresh trail led to the camp and John Thornton!

Buck hurried on softly. The forest was now still. The birds had flown away. The squirrels were all in hiding.

Buck sniffed the air. He followed a strong smell into some bushes. It was the smell of death! There lay Nig on his side, dead. In his body was a feathered arrow.

A hundred yards farther on, Buck found one of the sled dogs Thornton had got for the trip to the Lost Cabin Mine. The dog was not dead, but he soon would be. Buck passed him and went on toward camp.

From the camp he could hear the sound of many voices in a strange, singsong cry. Buck dropped to his belly and crawled to the clearing. Hans lay on his face, half a dozen feathered arrows in his back.

Buck looked toward the cabin. What he saw made his hair stand straight up. He growled a terrible wolf growl.

A band of Indians were dancing about the cabin. Suddenly they heard the howl of a wolf. A big dog who looked like a giant wolf was coming at them.

It was Buck. He threw himself at the Indians. He leaped at the nearest one, who happened to be the chief. He ripped the Indian chief's throat wide open. The blood poured over the man's chest. With a second leap Buck ripped open the throat of another Indian.

Nothing could stop Buck, and nothing could hold him. In and out among the Indians he tore, ripping and killing.

Buck was so terrible and so fast that the Indians' arrows could not find him. One young hunter threw a spear. It missed Buck and drove into the chest of another Indian. The Indians, thinking' that the gods had come to kill them, ran for the woods.

Buck seemed a devil in the form of a dog. He ran after them, dragging them down like deer as they raced through the woods. A few got away.

Buck ran back to camp. Pete had been killed in his bed when the Indians attacked. Buck found John Thornton's trail.

Buck followed his master's tracks into the deep pool of water. But there were no tracks leading away from the water. In the pool, hidden by the muddy water, lay John Thornton. Near the pool, head and feet in the water, lay Skeet, who must have tried to help his master.

All day Buck stayed at the pool. He knew John Thornton was dead. Something inside him hurt. He walked over and looked at the bodies of the Indians he had killed. He sniffed the bodies. After this, he would not be afraid of a man unless he had in his hands arrows, a spear, or a club.

Night came on. A full moon rose high over the trees into the sky. Beside the muddy pool lay Buck.

He rose sniffing. From far away he heard a faint, sharp cry. It was followed by other sharp yelps. As the moments passed, the yelps grew closer and louder. Buck walked to the clearing and listened.

He heard the call again. It was the same call he had heard before, sounding clearer than ever. Buck was ready to obey the call at last.

John Thornton was dead. The claims of love for a man no longer held Buck.

Hunting living meat to kill, the wolf pack had come at last to Buck's valley. Into the moonlit clearing they came. In the clearing Buck waited. At first, they were afraid. He seemed so big. Then one leaped for him.

Buck struck the wolf and broke his neck. Buck stood still, waiting. Three others tried it, one after another. And one after another, all three fell back, streaming blood.

Then the whole pack rushed forward together, to pull him down. Buck needed to be quick and sure. Turning on his hind legs, snapping and leaping, he was everywhere at once. So swiftly did he turn from side to side that they did not get him.

To keep the wolves from getting behind him, he was forced back, back. At last he came up against a high gravel bank.

There he stayed to fight to the death. The wolves could not sneak up in back or on the sides. Buck had to face only the front.

He fought well. At the end of half an hour, the wolves pulled back. Their tongues hung out, and their long white teeth flashed in the moonlight. Some lay down to rest. Others stood watching Buck. Some went down to lap water from the pool.

One wolf, long, lean, and gray, came toward Buck in a friendly way. Buck knew him. It was the wild brother. He was crying softly. Buck cried, and they touched noses.

Then an old wolf came forward. He was lean and scarred. Buck sniffed noses with him. At once the old wolf sat down. He pointed his nose at the moon and broke out in the long wolf howl.

The others sat down and howled also. And now Buck knew that this was indeed the call of the wild. Buck, too, sat down and howled.

Then Buck came out from the gravel bank. The wolf pack crowded around him. Half friendly, half wild, they sniffed. The leaders of the pack sprang away into the woods, yelping for the others to follow. The pack swung in behind them. Buck ran with them, yelping by the side of his wild brother.

This is the end of the story of Buck. A few years later, the Indians saw a change in the color of the timber wolves. Some were seen with splashes of brown on their heads and mouths. Some had white markings on their chests.

The Indians tell of the Ghost Dog that runs at the head of the wolf pack. They are afraid of this Ghost Dog, for it is wise and clever. It steals from their camps in the winters. It robs their traps and kills their dogs. It dares their bravest hunters.

Some hunters do not return to camp. They are found with their throats torn open. Prints around them in the snow are bigger than those of a wolf.

Each fall the Indians still follow the moose herd, but there is one valley they will not enter. In that valley, they say, live the bad spirits.

In the summers, one that the Indians do

not know about comes to that valley. It is a great wolf, a wolf like all others, yet unlike them. He crosses alone from the timber land. He comes down into an open clearing.

Here a yellow stream of gold flows to the ground from rotted moosehide sacks. Long grass grows around the yellow gold, hiding it from the sun.

Here the great wolf stays alone for a time. Before he leaves, he howls once, long and sadly.

But he is not always alone. When the long winter nights come on, the wolves follow their meat down into the lower valleys. This one may be seen running at the head of the pack. He leaps like a giant above the other wolves.

It is Buck, the leader of the wolf pack. He has answered the call of the wild.

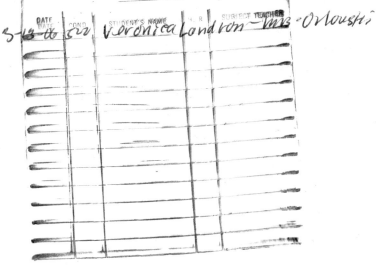

PROPERTY OF THE CITY OF PASSAIC

PASSAIC SENIOR HIGH SCHOOL

PASSAIC, NEW JERSEY

No. **53** Year **99**

Damage beyond ordinary wear must be paid for. If rendered useless, or if lost, the book must be paid for before another book is placed in the pupil's hand.

By order of the Passaic Board of Education

PLEASE PRINT

DATE	COND.	STUDENT'S NAME	H. R.	SUBJECT TEACHER
3-13-00	522	Veronica Londron	MB	Orloushi

Phoenix Everyreaders

ROBIN HOOD STORIES
KING ARTHUR AND HIS KNIGHTS
THE TROJAN WAR
GREEK AND ROMAN MYTHS
INDIAN PAINT
WILD ANIMALS I HAVE KNOWN
BOB, SON OF BATTLE
THE CALL OF THE WILD
THE GOLD BUG AND OTHER STORIES
CASES OF SHERLOCK HOLMES
MEN OF IRON
BEN HUR
THE SILVER SKATES
TREASURE ISLAND
KIDNAPPED
A TALE OF TWO CITIES

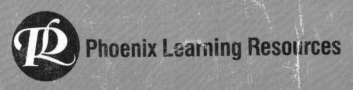

Phoenix Learning Resources

ISBN 0-7915-1363-

DATE	COND.	STUDENT'S NAME	H. R.	SUBJECT TEACHER
3-13-06	522	Veronica Londron — MB ·Orloushi		

Phoenix Everyreaders

ROBIN HOOD STORIES
KING ARTHUR AND HIS KNIGHTS
THE TROJAN WAR
GREEK AND ROMAN MYTHS
INDIAN PAINT
WILD ANIMALS I HAVE KNOWN
BOB, SON OF BATTLE
THE CALL OF THE WILD
THE GOLD BUG AND OTHER STORIES
CASES OF SHERLOCK HOLMES
MEN OF IRON
BEN HUR
THE SILVER SKATES
TREASURE ISLAND
KIDNAPPED
A TALE OF TWO CITIES

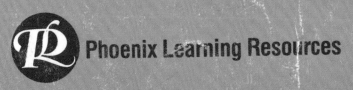 Phoenix Learning Resources

ISBN 0–7915–1363–